TOO FAST

Douglas Maxwell

TOO FAST

OBERON BOOKS
LONDON

WWW.OBERONBOOKS.COM

First published in 2011 by Oberon Books Ltd
521 Caledonian Road, London N7 9RH
Tel: +44 (0) 20 7607 3637 / Fax: +44 (0) 20 7607 3629
e-mail: info@oberonbooks.com
www.oberonbooks.com

A catalogue record for this book is available from the British Library.

ISBN: 978-1-84943-125-5

Members of Scarborough Youth Theatre performing *Too Fast* at the National Theatre. Image: Simon Annand.

Printed and bound by CPI Group (UK) Ltd, Croydon, CR0 4YY.

Contents

Characters

Spoke's Brother
(M) 13/14 yrs old

DD
(F) 14-16 yrs old

Amee
(F) 14-16 yrs old

Sean
(M) 14-16 yrs old

Marcy
(F) 14-16 yrs old

Young Jean Brown
(F) 13/14 yrs old

Nadia
(F) 13/14 yrs old

Callum Hunt
(M) 16-18 yrs old

Laila
(F) 16-18 yrs old

Frankie Tear
(F) 16-18 yrs old

Jake Spence
(M) 16-18 yrs old

Ali Monroe
(F) 16-18 yrs old

Too Fast was performed by Scarborough Youth Theatre as part of the NT Connections Festival on Wednesday 29 June 2011 in the Cottesloe, National Theatre, London.

This play is set – for the most part – in the side room of a church. At the moment the room is being used for storage.

It's a dusty, unloved place; crammed with broken statues, unwanted crosses, dated Jesus paintings, wonky baptismal fonts, stacks of hard seats, mammoth candle sticks and a group of very uncomfortable-looking young people in school uniform.

There's a door at the back which opens out onto the congregation and another less obvious entrance/exit which is curtained off and leads down a corridor.

It's a cold room and there's a thin-ice, backstage, pre-show atmosphere.

To one side is SPOKE'S BROTHER. He's not with the others – they can't be doing with him. He's a bit younger than them too. Maybe thirteen or fourteen. And he's talking. He knows no other way.

All the others in the room are between fourteen and sixteen years old and part of Sensation Nation, a choir/singing group led by DD. Sensation Nation is DD's baby and when Britain's Got Talent *comes back she swears to god they're going to be huge man. She's nervous though. This will be their début, and it's a different kind of gig altogether.*

They're here to sing at a funeral.

AMEE has the best voice in Sensation Nation. She's not officially second in command, but something about her (the accent?) means that her opinion carries a bit of weight. For all that though, she's not too bothered about Sensation Nation really.

SEAN's stealing looks at AMEE while pretending to fiddle with his phone. He's a bit confused. It's all a bit vague exactly how SEAN ended up in Sensation Nation. Or how he ended up with DD and not AMEE. Or how they ended up at this girl's funeral singing in front of the whole school – the whole world it seems like. Or how…yeah; everything's a bit vague and confusing for SEAN.

MARCY keeps a lookout at the door. She's providing an excited commentary on who's on the pews. God it's going to be huge this. Everyone's here. Mind you the dead girl was only young. People love that.

NADIA is DD's biggest fan. She's DD's shadow; her Mini-Me-Rottweiler.

She's working hard to get her moves down: the turned-up face and folded arms, the tuts, the struts, the hair flicks. She's a good bit younger than DD but she's working on that too.

In fact NADIA's in the same year as YOUNG JEAN BROWN. A small, almost silent girl who looks mouse-like and insular. When YOUNG JEAN BROWN speaks she tends to get a reaction.

Later on we'll meet some older pupils. They will be between sixteen and eighteen. They're friends of the girl that died.

We'll meet CALLUM HUNT, an intimidating guy who has taken it upon himself to ensure that this day will be a fitting and respectable tribute, even if he has to break a few heads to make it happen.

We'll meet LAILA, DD's big sister – bursting bubbles in that delighted, older siblings way.

And we'll meet FRANKIE, the dead girl's best pal and a school celebrity (a goddess, DD would say) after an unsuccessful appearance on X-Factor. She's only just recovered from that debacle, and now this.

They will be looking for JAKE SPENCE. Keeping an eye out. JAKE's not welcome here. The dead girl's mum and dad said that if he dared show his face…

Why?

Didn't you hear? See, when the ambulance got to the crash and found her body trapped in that mangled can of a car…they didn't find JAKE.

Because JAKE ran away. JAKE left her. He left his girlfriend there to die.

Poor ALI.

We'll meet her later too.

But that's to come. Right now it's just the members of Sensation Nation, and SPOKE'S BROTHER. And he's <u>still</u> talking. It looks like they've been listening to him talk for a long, long time…

SPOKE'S BROTHER: I'll tell you another children's programme that's all about death. I said I'll tell you another children's programme that's all about death.

Nothing.

SPOKE'S BROTHER: *In the Night Garden.* Yup. *In The Night Garden* is all about death.

SEAN: What's *In The Night Garden?*

DD: Sean!

SEAN: What?

DD: What did I just say?

SEAN: When?

DD: Just there. Don't engage with him.

NADIA: She's only just said it there Sean!

SEAN: I'm not engaging with him, I'm asking him a question.

DD: That's engaging.

NADIA: That's what engaging *is* Sean. God sake.

DD: Just keep focused. Right? Everyone. It's enough we have to listen to Young Jean Brown here constantly spouting filth every single minute of the day without him distracting us with all his Cbeebies death-show stuff. This is too important to… *(Deep breath.)* Focus on your parts, focus on your breathing and before we know it…we'll be…Just everybody focus! *(To MARCY.)* Anything?

MARCY: No. The front ones are still empty. But there's about a million people crammed in down the sides. Can't be long now. It's so quiet. All you can hear is Callum Hunt telling people where to sit and even that's a whisper.

SEAN: I hate Callum Hunt.

MARCY: *(Not listening.)* He's so mature isn't he? All those little nods and telling people where to sit. He's like a real live proper person. He's better at this than the teachers. Old Blades was crying right, and Callum whatdoyomacalled him…rectified him. Right there in front of everybody. It was very impressive.

AMEE: Yeah, I'm not sure rectified is the right word Marcy.

MARCY: Well he put his arm round him and everything.

AMEE: Yeah but…

SEAN: I hate Callum Hunt.

MARCY: You wouldn't say that if he was telling you where to sit Sean. You would be very impressed.

SEAN: I'd be impressed if he apologised, but that's never going to happen.

AMEE: Apologised for what?

SEAN: I can't talk about it Amee. *(Beat.)* Once, like, for no reason, he grabbed me from a swing, rubbed my head in nettles and then tied my shoes to the tail of a stunt kite. For no reason.

AMEE: Aaaaw.

SEAN: I know. I remember thinking at the time, 'oh my god'.

DD: Right that's another thing, we can't cry. That's very important everyone. Okay? No crying. If *we* cry *they* won't – and we want them to cry. That's a vote-winner.

NADIA: No crying.

DD: Just remember…

NADIA: She was going too fast, it was her own fault.

Pause.

DD gives NADIA a Sergeant Major's glare before continuing…

DD: Just remember…Let the song do the work. That's what Simon Cowell says and I for one listen to Simon after everything he's achieved in the industry. I give Simon a lot of respect. And could everybody please, *please* just…focus.

No more talking. I don't want to boss people about but that is actually an order.

Pause. They go back to doing whatever it was they were…

SEAN: What's *In The Night Garden*?

AMEE: It's like *Teletubbies.* My little sister is addicted to it. All babies are. It's like baby heroin. And okay, it might be a bit freaky, but it's not about death. It's all teddies and toys, all like totally hugging in a forest and stuff.

SEAN: I don't get it.

AMEE: *(Teasing.)* Yeah it's a bit complicated for you Sean. If you like I can get one of my sister's picture books and we can work on it a page at a time and…

SEAN: *(Pretending to be offended, but really delighted.)* Hey, that's not what I…I mean I don't get how it's all about…Oh my god I can't believe you would…cheek man…!

SEAN playfully punches AMEE who squeals a bit. They toy fight a little. DD (and NADIA) are not amused…

DD: Excuse me. Excuse me!

NADIA: *(Viciously.)* Excuse me!

SEAN and AMEE stop.

NADIA: *(Disgusted.)* For god sake.

DD: I'm sorry Sean if this isn't important to you, but, you know what I mean?

SEAN: Sorry DD.

DD: Maybe you don't want to be in Sensation Nation any more is that it?

SEAN: Well…no it's…

DD: Maybe you don't want to have the honour of performing a poor dead girl's favourite song in front of the whole school and be a total legend, is that it?

SEAN: Well…no it's…

DD: Or maybe you don't want to be my life partner anymore then. Is that it?

SEAN: …

DD: You and 'Amee' now is it? Maybe you and 'Amee' would rather just watch Sensation Nation win next year's *Britain's Got Talent* from the comfort of your own home? Is that what this is? Is that what you would both prefer?

Em…yes.

NADIA: No! That's preposterous.

SEAN: No I was only…sort of…Sorry DD.

AMEE: Sorry DD.

DD: Whatever. Can I just ask a question…and this is for everyone…

SPOKE'S BROTHER: Me too?

DD: No, just them. Who is it that runs Sensation Nation? Who actually *is* Sensation Nation?

General mumbles from the group. NADIA helps out by pointing at DD.

DD: Pardon?

NADIA: Pardon?

Everyone responds now: 'you' 'DD' 'you are' etc.

DD: That's right. It's a collective. We're doing this for each other. We need to work together guys. Come on. *(Pointedly at AMEE.)* As the saying goes: this is no time to drive wedges between life partners just so you get to do more solos. Know what I mean?

MARCY: *(Back at the door peeking out.)* Aw. He's ruffling their hair now. He's ruffling their hair and they're loving it. It's cheering them right up. Aw. Bless.

AMEE: He's ruffling the teachers' hair?

MARCY: No, the little kids. There's a whole class of little kids coming in. Don't know who they are. Why would someone bring little kids to this?

AMEE: It'll be her brother's class. Her brother's only six.

MARCY: Still. It's a bit brazen.

AMEE: Brazen?

MARCY: *(Snippy.)* Yes Amee. Brazen. This isn't your old school you know. We don't play Quidditch and wear hats here. We speak normal us so desist it up.

SEAN: He's ruffling hair now, but just watch: in five minutes' time he'll have their shoes on the tail of a stunt kite doing loop the loops. Then the shoes will fall into a garden and there'll be a big dog in that garden and they'll have to walk home in their socks and they'll get into bad, bad trouble. God I hate Callum Hunt.

SPOKE'S BROTHER has his hand up. NADIA points this out to DD. Reluctantly…

DD: Yes?

SPOKE'S BROTHER: Children need to know about death. It's what separates us from the animals. Even blue whales think they're immortal. That's what's so great about *In The Night Garden*. It might look like toys cuddling in a forest but what it's really saying is that everyone has to face up to death someday. Everyone. Little kids *should* be here.

DD: We're not talking about this now thank you.

AMEE: *(To SPOKE'S BROTHER.)* Yeah but *In The Night Garden* isn't about any of that.

DD: We're not talking about this now Amee.

AMEE: Just a minute…

AMEE holds her finger up to DD.

NADIA gasps at the outrageous insubordination. DD keeps up appearances for the benefit of the group with a tolerating smile.

AMEE: *(Continuing.)* It's not about death – that's absurd. It's toys in a forest going goo goo ga ga. It's for babies. Trust me, I've seen it a million times man.

SPOKE'S BROTHER: Well then you'll know it starts with Iggle Piggle lost at sea. 'In a boat, no bigger than my hand, out on the ocean, far away from land'. Right? And what does he do? 'He takes his little sail down'. Down! Iggle Piggle is ready to die, when, above him, all the stars in the sky turn into flowers and suddenly he's in a garden. And yes, there are toys there and yes he does play – one last time. But soon they all go to sleep – Upsy Daisy, The Tombliboos, The Pontipines; they all sleep. All of them *except* Iggle Piggle. Because Iggle Piggle has to live. And do you remember what the last line is? 'Don't worry Iggle Piggle, it's time to go'. It's time to *go!* Not sleep, not die, but *go.* To accept death and live! Living, fighting, trying! And so he does – he leaves the garden and goes back to his ship, sailing from sight, forward on the tide, into the now.

JEAN BROWN: Fuck *off!*

DD: *(Raging.)* Hey! What did I say!? What did I say about swearing!? We could get pulled from the gig if the church people hear that. Church people go ballisto at swearing. Swearing is the worst thing anyone can do at this moment in time. Sometimes I think you're a saboteur Young Jean Brown. Know that? See if I find out you're trying to destroy Sensation Nation from within then…oh…know what I mean.

NADIA: *(Right into YJB's face.)* I will fight you.

Another pause.

AMEE: What's he doing here anyway?

SEAN: That's Spoke's Brother.

DD: He's doing the reading. Don't engage.

AMEE: *(To SPOKE's BROTHER.)* You're doing the reading? How'd you swing that?

SPOKE'S BROTHER: *(Different.)* I knew her.

*   *   *

A little time has passed.

Sensation Nation are all crowded around the door, trying to get a glimpse of what's going on in the congregation. AMEE is stuck right at the back and can't see anything. SPOKE'S BROTHER is where he was before.

AMEE: What's happening?

MARCY: Callum Hunt shook their hands and hugged the mum. It was amazing and now they're all kind of…walking down to their seats in clutches. There's a troop of them. Cousins must be. Her dad's still at the back though. He's not moving. Oh – he is now. He's like, gripping onto the seats though. It's like he's on a boat or…like he's going to fall down. No. Don't fall down. Don't fall man please. They've got him. No. He's shrugged them off. It's just him again. He wants to do it on his own I think. And now he's…just…kind of…just…just…disintegrating.

AMEE: I don't think you mean disintegrating.

The crowd parts to let her see for herself.

No. Disintegrating was right.

Soon they don't want to look at that anymore. They go back to their places.

After ages…

DD: Right. Em. We need to put that out of our minds. Focus. Breathe. It won't be long now. Talk about something else.

Nothing springs to mind.

DD Talk about something else I said.

This seems to be directed at NADIA, who struggles a bit. Then…

NADIA: Em…what's *Postman Pat* all about?

DD: What?

NADIA: What's *Postman Pat* about? You know. Is it about dying or something? I wonder.

DD: Nadia, *Postman Pat* is about a Postman. Called Pat.

NADIA: Oh yeah. So it is. Good point DD.

SPOKE'S BROTHER: It's not actually.

DD: I swear to god man…

SPOKE'S BROTHER: There's a Postman in it, and he is called Pat but that's not what it's about.

AMEE: No no no. You can't get us on this one. We've *all* seen *Postman Pat* and we all know it's definitely nothing to do with death.

SPOKE'S BROTHER: Didn't say it was about death. *Postman Pat* is about how everyone has to tell themselves that they're happy even if they're not. You've got to put on a show, find a happy song to sing, or how can anything change?

AMEE: Where are you getting this crap from?

SPOKE'S BROTHER: It's all in the song. 'Pat thinks he's a really happy man'. He's not *actually* happy – he just 'thinks' he is. He has to tell himself all's well everyday or he'll notice that his life is a humdrum shambles and he'll fall apart.

SEAN: Shut up! Pat's life is not a shambles!

SPOKE'S BROTHER: Well, everything's a mess underneath innit? I don't see why Pat should be any different. People are always saying that in a village with only one ginger-haired man, there are a great many ginger-haired children running about. So it could be that.

SEAN: No this isn't right.

DD: Sean do not engage with…

SEAN: It's not 'Pat thinks he's a really happy man'. It's 'Pat *feels* he's a really happy man'.

SPOKE'S BROTHER: That's the same thing.

SEAN: Thinking and feeling is not the same.

SPOKE'S BROTHER: In this case there's very little difference in the words.

SEAN: They're opposites.

SPOKE'S BROTHER: They sound like opposites but the ultimate meaning is the same. Like em…like…

JEAN BROWN: Like a guy who's a dick but at the same time is also a fanny?

SPOKE'S BROTHER: Yeah. Pardon?

DD: *(To YJB.)* One more from you! One more!

NADIA: *(To YJB.)* One more I swear to god!

SEAN: Nah I'm not having this. He's a lovely guy Postman Pat. A really lovely guy. And I hate it when people say his life is a shambles and he's got loads of other kids. Because sometimes right, when I'm in on my own I watch *Postman Pat.* I don't care. Nah, I don't care. And yeah, it's for little ones but it's wonderful and everything. I like the colours. The colours sort of remind me of when it wasn't shit and stuff. Know what I mean? When it wasn't all pressure and…shit. And for that ten minutes I'm back again. When it was alright. You know? And I sing the song. I do, I sing it. And even when I'm not watching it, sometimes I sing it. If things are turning wrong and my guts are all tight and sore, I sing it. Know what I mean? And for as long as the song lasts I'm alright. So leave him alone. Yeah? He's not like all the others. And I am telling you, it is, definitely, 100 per cent, 'Pat *feels* he's a very happy man'. I'm singing it in my head now. 'Feels'.

There's a big pause.

Someone – who I wonder? – starts to hum the Postman Pat theme. After a bit some others join in.

It does actually help. They're feeling better.

Soon they're all humming. Even DD.

It gets louder and louder. They hum a couple of verses and the middle bit.

They're having fun. The next time the verse comes round they start to sing. MARCY has moved away from the door to join in.

They feel good. They feel like children. They sing…

ALL: Postman Pat

Postman Pat

Postman Pat and his black and white cat.

Early in the morning

Just as day is dawning

Pat thinks/feels…

CALLUM HUNT explodes through the door in a fury. Everyone jumps and stops singing; except SEAN who has his back to the door and carries on happily with 'he's a really happy man!' until…

CALLUM grabs him and wrestles him to the floor.

This has happened in seconds and the shock of it has everyone else frozen and staring.

SEAN, in a panic, tries to kick CALLUM off but CALLUM grabs his foot and roughly removes his shoe.

SEAN: Not the shoes! Oh my god! Not the shoes!

CALLUM gets the other one off and after battering SEAN with them a couple of times he throws them into the corner of the room over by the curtained exit, goes to the main door and shuts it, then rounds on the rest in a terrifying stage whisper...

CALLUM: This...is...a...funeral! Have...some...fucking...*respect!*

SEAN: *(From the floor.)* I don't believe it. It's my worst nightmare came true. Again!

CALLUM: Is he in charge? Is this the leader?

SPOKE'S BROTHER: It's a collective.

CALLUM: I beg your pardon ballbag?

NADIA: I'm the leader. It's my shoes you want.

DD: No. It's not. She's not. And neither's he. I'm the leader. Although technically it *is* actually a collective but I organise the...

CALLUM: Then you're coming with me girl. Right now! You're bloody lucky Keith got carted off to get some holy water splashed on his face and missed your little flashback singalong or you'd be in even worse trouble. But everyone else caught it. So you're coming with me to apologise to the whole church. Now!

DD: What? But we were just...

AMEE: Warming up...

Together.

DD: Nervous.

AMEE: *(Cont.)* And anyway how is our singing any worse than you battering people with shoes?

NADIA: And swearing. We're not swearing. Swearing is the worst thing anyone can do at this moment in time.

DD: Nadia just…

CALLUM: Worst thing anyone can do? Oh yeah. Right. Okay then, when you're out there grovelling why don't you ask Ali's mum and dad and all those weeping teachers what the worst thing anyone can do is? Do you think they'll say 'swearing'? Or 'slapping some dunce with a shoe?' Do you? I don't.

NADIA: Church people really hate swearing though.

CALLUM: Worse than killing someone?

NADIA: Worse than singing *Postman Pat.*

SPOKE'S BROTHER: He didn't kill her though.

A couple of big beats.

Well. He didn't.

CALLUM shifts his gaze to SPOKE's BROTHER, who immediately realises that he's made a mistake…

CALLUM: Who says he didn't? Who says?

SPOKE'S BROTHER: She…she was killed…in the crash. Immediately.

CALLUM: You know that for a fact do you? Well do you? You were in the car with her when she left the party were you? Hey, I said were you?

SPOKE'S BROTHER: No.

CALLUM: No. But who was? Who was?

SPOKE'S BROTHER: Jake Spence.

CALLUM: And who was in the car with her when she lost control and skidded off the road?

SPOKE'S BROTHER: Jake Spence.

CALLUM: And who was in the car when the ambulance arrived and found her dead at the wheel?

SPOKE'S BROTHER: Jake Spe…

CALLUM: Wrong! Wrong. Jake Spence was *not* with her when the ambulance arrived because Jake Spence had bolted. Jake Spence had run a mile. He left her there to save himself. His own girlfriend. We know *that* for a fact. And the police know it. And the papers know it. Everyone out there knows it. But what we don't know is exactly when she died. Because no one was there to see it. And that's a crime as bad as killing in my eyes. The worst thing anyone could do. End of.

Pause.

MARCY: God you're so impressive Callum.

CALLUM: What?

MARCY: Nothing. I'm just saying you're like, really impressive. The way you speak, the way you behave out there. The nods, the whispers…

JEAN BROWN: The beatings.

MARCY: If ever you like, want to…?

CALLUM: What?

MARCY: Well. I dunno. Anything. With me. I would. I don't mean…I'm talking about ice skating really. Or playing something on the Wii. Just hang out. I mean…you probably don't. Want to. You definitely don't. Sorry. Just. For god sake I'm only joking!

CALLUM laughs in her face. Shakes his head in disbelief. MARCY shrinks away to nothing.

CALLUM: You bloody babies. *(To DD.)* Right – c'mon.

DD: Where?

CALLUM: Out there. People need to see justice.

DD: What, apologise? Seriously? To…what, to everyone?

CALLUM: Today.

DD doesn't move.

AMEE: You're in no position to demand apologies. You owe Sean an apology and look at him: still waiting. And anyway who says you're in charge?

CALLUM: Keith. The dad. In their kitchen two days ago. 'You're a good lad Callum. Any trouble at the funeral you know what to do.' Exact quote from the dad. Postman Pat was trouble, he was the principle Pat singer, I knew what to do: shoe justice to the chest and arms. End of. No apology needed.

AMEE: I'm not talking about Pat. I'm talking about the stunt kite incident. You tied his shoes to a stunt kite and you've never even said sorry. Not once.

CALLUM: What? When was this?

AMEE: When was this Sean?

SEAN: *(Sheepishly.)* Oh I dunno. I can't really remember Amee. My birthday I think. May the 2nd 2001 or something. About three o'clock or something. I dunno. Quarter past three. Or something. I dunno.

AMEE: May the 2nd 2001. Three-ish.

CALLUM: I'm not apologising for something I'm meant to've done on May the fucking 2nd 2001. Christ I was only… what, nine?

SEAN: Yeah, I was six. I always remember it was my sixth birthday cos that was the birthday I got my shoes eaten by a big dog.

AMEE: If you apologise we'll apologise. That's justice.

CALLUM: Nah, nah, nah That's out of order. No-one blames kids for the stupid shit they done when they were kids.

That's the rule. Kids do stupid shit but then one day they stop doing stupid shit, all is forgiven, and that's us grown up. That's life in a nutshell. No apology necessary. Justice does not apply. And anyway how can you fly a stunt kite with a six year old moron tied to it? It's just not believable.

SEAN: No, I wasn't wearing the shoes at the time. They'd been yanked off.

CALLUM: You're yanking me off right now son. This is bullshit.

DD: *(Faking confidence.)* Look…We're still singing the song. You can't stop us.

CALLUM: What song?

DD: We're Sensation Nation.

SPOKE'S BROTHER: I'm not.

DD: He's not. The rest of us are though. We're singing her favourite song as the coffin gets carried out. Miss Ronson said we were all to wait here until we heard the cue. We're still doing it. Aren't we? Apology or no apology. You can't stop us. Actually. It's all arranged and everything.

CALLUM: Well tough luck girl cos I'm going to unarrange it just as soon as…wait a minute. Hold on. *Postman Pat* was Ali's favourite song?

DD: No.

SPOKE'S BROTHER: *(Pointing at SEAN.)* It's his favourite song.

SEAN: No it's not.

CALLUM: Why you singing his favourite song as the coffin gets carried out? He's a little pussy.

SEAN: It's not my favourite song.

CALLUM: What's he even got to do with it? He didn't even know her.

DD: We're not singing his favourite song…

SEAN: It's *one* of my favourite songs…

DD: We're singing this.

DD hands over a lyric sheet.

CALLUM: This isn't her favourite song either. Nah, you should've asked me. I'd've told you. This'll be shit.

NADIA: *(Snatching it back.)* No it won't. We've practised it. DD's done the arrangement and it's beautiful and everyone'll cry cos it's beautiful and we do this really cool thing.

CALLUM: Should've got some of us older ones to do it. Frankie Tear should've done it. She's been on X Factor and everything, what've you ever done? Okay she was shit but at least she was Ali's real mate – wouldn't be barging in on it like all you lambs.

AMEE: We didn't barge in on it.

CALLUM: Well you weren't invited. I know who was invited. How come you're doing the song if you didn't even know her and weren't invited?

Good point. The rest of Sensation Nation hadn't thought about that. Their gaze slowly turns to DD who's avoiding eyes.

DD: What? *(Beat.)* We were invited. We were. *(Beat.)* Eventually. Kind of.

AMEE: DD…

DD: Look we got the gig didn't we? This is our début, it's been decided and it's perfect. This is the sad story we spring from – they'll show us wiping away tears in slow motion if we get to the semis. Springing from a sad story is the ultimate vote winner. No one can say this isn't a total opportunity.

AMEE: Yeah but how did we get invited if we didn't…?

DD: As the saying goes, 'sometimes, in order for good things to happen, some people have to tell some other people lies.' End of.

CALLUM: You lied to Keith? Ooooooh. This is trouble. Justice is coming.

AMEE: DD! Did you lie to Keith?

DD: No! I lied to my sister and she lied to Keith. But she didn't know she was lying so there's really no need to tell her. Laila's weird, she gets angry about stuff like that. Look, all I said was that Ali was a member of Sensation Nation and one of her last wishes was to hear us sing. Which is a *white* lie really cos I have actually made her an honorary member since she died.

SEAN: Since she died? What, like a ghost?

DD: Sean…

AMEE: Oh my God we've totally crashed this.

DD: The whole world's crashed it Amee. You think every weeper out there knew Ali Monroe? No way. But they're all here aren't they? All dressed up and gawping. Well we're contributing. That's the difference. We're helping, know what I mean? We're offering her something. Something good.

SPOKE'S BROTHER: She's right. You are doing something nice for Ali. She loved music, she would've loved this. It *is* good.

AMEE: It's based on a lie though.

DD: So what? If it ends in something beautiful so what? This isn't a random thing you know – I've worked at this, planned it out. You don't understand how these programmes work, I do. When we go on the show it's all about layers and storylines. New things have to crop up to keep the voters interested week by week or we're dead. It's not all about singing. For some people, who, you know, can't sing as well as you, it can't be about singing at all. That's why I've layered our story. Why do you think I picked this particular group of people for Sensation Nation? Singing skills? Yeah right. We can learn that. No. There are other reasons. Believe me.

Pause.

CALLUM: What other reasons?

DD: What's it to you?

CALLUM: Dunno. Interested.

AMEE: So am I. What other reasons DD?

DD: Well. Look, you're a really good singer. And we need a really good singer. I'm a really good leader and we need a really good leader. Know what I mean?

MARCY: What am I then? Why did you pick me?

DD: *(This is all difficult.)* You're…well…you know… *(Sigh.)* Remember the time when we were at that Geography conference and the seats caught fire and you said to me that you totally hated Amee? Well I thought…if you fell out during the heats it wouldn't be the worst thing in the world. Tension is a vote winner and so is someone walking out. Don't make the face Marcy everyone has a role. Young Jean Brown is the rotten-looking one that they can make-over and who'll get better and better as the series goes on. That's her role and she's not complaining.

SEAN: Oh no. Don't tell me. Don't tell me you only picked me cos we're going out? Did you? DD? Is that the only reason I'm here? Kissing ability? Is it?

DD: No. Of course that's not the only reason Sean. You've also got learning difficulties. And after Susan Boyle, that's more important than ever. So that's two reasons.

SEAN: Oh my god!

DD: I'm sorry Sean. But it doesn't change the fact that I really love you or whatever.

SEAN: I don't have learning difficulties DD.

DD: Oh come on Sean you do.

SEAN: I don't though.

DD: Yes Sean, you do.

NADIA: DD? DD? Can I em…ask? Why em…why me? What's my role? I wonder.

DD: Well. Well. You're poor aren't you?

NADIA: *(Devastated.)* Oh. Yeah. Yeah. Okay.

DD: I don't think I've done anything wrong. I really don't.

Pause. The room disagrees.

SEAN: Hands up who thinks I've got learning difficulties.

CALLUM puts his hand up. No one else does.

From outside the door the organ plays.

SPOKE'S BROTHER: It's starting.

The door opens and LAILA and FRANKIE come in. LAILA looks all keyed up and FRANKIE looks terrible – the shadow of her former self.

CALLUM: *(Straightening his tie.)* I know. I'm coming, I'm coming. *(Threatening the others.)* Later.

LAILA: Jake's back.

CALLUM: What?

LAILA: Jake. Frankie saw him didn't you Frankie?

FRANKIE: He was running round the side of the church…he was…he was hiding but yeah, it was definitely him.

LAILA: Callum…Jake Spence is here.

*   *   *

Some more time has passed.

We can hear the drone of the service next door. For the first time we can see that the wall and ceiling of this room is covered in a faded mural. From what we can make out behind the piles of cluttered and damaged church stuff, it's of the moon and the stars – the heavens I suppose. The style is ancient, ornate; though the details are lost, the paint faded.

Sensation Nation – apart from SEAN who's over in the corner looking for his shoes – are gathered in a huddle. Very, very quietly they're warming up. DD hums a note and the others match it, then harmonize.

It doesn't last – fizzles out. The group's heart isn't in it. They feel used and sad. They wish they weren't here. DD probably knows that Sensation Nation is over.

SPOKE's BROTHER, CALLUM, LAILA and FRANKIE aren't here.

After a moment…

DD: *(Without her previous authority)* We have to warm up.

AMEE: Why?

DD: If we want to be good…

MARCY: Who says we want to be good?

DD: The whole school is…We have to do the song. It's a funeral. We don't have a choice. Imagine if we don't sing?

MARCY: I imagine you'd be desolated. Is that the right word Amee?

AMEE: *(Not malicious.)* Yeah. I think it is Marcy.

SEAN: How can shoes just disappear man? They're nowhere! It's like, if Derren Brown worked in a shoe shop this is what would happen. Absolutely no work would get done. Can someone please help me look?

He gets no response.

DD: We've got to sing. It doesn't matter about *Britain's Got Talent* or anything, but we've got to sing today.

MARCY: Maybe you should sing on your own then DD? I'm sure everyone will be moved by your beautiful leadership skills.

DD: I can't sing on my own.

MARCY: Why not?

DD: I'm not…I'm not good enough.

MARCY: Well that's a shame.

SEAN: They have just simply vanished. They were here one minute then that Arsehole Hunt has somehow lobbed them into a parallel universe. I need shoes man. I'm just not myself without shoes on. Help me look someone! I can't see the shoes for the trees here man!

The door opens and SPOKE'S BROTHER comes in. He's just done his reading. He goes to close the door but FRANKIE bustles in after him, followed by LAILA. FRANKIE is upset and finds some space away from the others. LAILA comforts her a bit.

FRANKIE: I'm alright. I was just, you know. Drowning a bit. *(About SPOKE's BROTHER.)* I saw him come in and…

LAILA: It's okay.

FRANKIE: I thought it'd be another world in here or something. God. Sorry.

LAILA: It's okay. It's just my little sister and that. They don't know anything about anything.

SPOKE'S BROTHER: Wait a minute. What the hell am I doing back in here? I was supposed to go and sit with my mum and dad! Sake. Oh well. Would you all like to know how it went? Would it be useful if I describe, in detail, my recent experiences? To give you, you know, an idea of what awaits you on the other side?

Beat.

AMEE: Maybe we should help Sean look for his shoes?

Yeah the group agree that they'd rather do that than listen to SPOKE's BROTHER. He doesn't seem to mind the fact that they all turn away and start a half-hearted hunt through the room. He continues as if they were rapt…

SPOKE'S BROTHER: Yeah it went okay actually. Nervous though see *(His hands are shaking.)* I was alright until I looked up. They're even standing outside, all the way up the gravel to the graveyard. And there's speakers out there so everyone can hear. But a stand must've broken or something because Mr Gibbons is up on a plastic chair, holding a speaker in both hands, like this. I thought, god, whatever I say next will vibrate in his arms. It'll go all the way back to the graves. And when I looked back down at the reading I couldn't make out the words anymore. I could see them, but as like, marks on paper, not as real words with meanings. I heard someone say 'poor kid'. But I wasn't upset. Well, not until then. Cos then, after that, the meanings kind of came into focus. And now it *did* seem sad. Sad that all these words – every word from now on in – will vibrate nowhere near Ali. And I thought 'Poor Kid'. But I just read it. Without thinking or feeling or meaning or anything. And got off. I concentrated on not tripping and anyway, it went okay apart from, you know, coming back in here.

Pause. During his speech, one by one they stopped looking for SEAN's shoes and started to listen to what he was saying. After a bit…

MARCY: What about Jake Spence?

SPOKE'S BROTHER: Dunno.

LAILA: He won't show. No way. He knows what would happen.

SPOKE'S BROTHER: Callum Hunt and all them – they're going in and out, down the aisles, watching at the door. It'll be all their birthdays if he does show.

LAILA: It makes no sense for him to show.

MARCY: Yeah but maybe he's drunk? Or on drugs. I heard he's a mess. Everyone says he was on drugs the night they crashed. That's *why* they crashed my mum says.

FRANKIE: He wasn't on drugs. Neither was Ali. She'd never done anything. And now she never will so tell your mum to relax.

LAILA: Don't let them get to you Frankie, they're just little kids.

FRANKIE: Must be nice. To be a little kid again. I didn't know how good it was, did you? It was gone so quick. I remember the day right, the exact day it went. I was in the garden, playing with this doll I had, my favourite one and I just…couldn't do it anymore. I felt dumb. Watched. It was gone.

LAILA: Do you want me to get my mum?

DD: Is mum here?

LAILA: Everyone's here.

DD: Is dad here?

LAILA: Of course not. Frankie, do you want me to get my mum?

FRANKIE: What are you all doing? Why are you all here?

LAILA: It's DD' s little singing thing. They're doing a song. It's nothing. You don't need to go back to Ali's house if you don't want to. I'll tell them you're not feeling well.

FRANKIE: *(To DD.)* You're going to sing?

DD: Well. We were going to, but it all got kind of…

JEAN BROWN: Fucked.

DD: Yeah. Would you like to sing Frankie? You know the song. You'd be amazing.

DD hands her the lyric sheet.

FRANKIE: This is her favourite. Was. Is.

DD: You'd be amazing.

FRANKIE: No I wouldn't.

DD: That's why I'm, know what I mean. Doing it. Cos of you on X Factor. I couldn't believe it.

FRANKIE: Right.

DD: Cos no one in this place ever does anything. None of them. They just sit back and jeer and do nothing. But you did. You showed them. Didn't you?

FRANKIE: Yeah. I showed them. Showed them how shit and desperate and scared someone could be. And the funny thing is I asked for it too, didn't I? Queued up and begged for it. I was at my worst. And now everything I touch… absolutely everything is exactly as bad as I was that night. And always will be.

DD: No you were great. Wasn't she? She was amazing wasn't she?

No one responds. Until…

NADIA: Yeah. I thought you were amazing.

DD: The very next day I decided, 'right, I'm getting a group together'. If Frankie Tear can do it I can. You were my inspiration. That's why I'm doing this.

LAILA: I thought you were doing this so dad could see you on TV?

DD: No.

LAILA: DD thinks just cos Dad met his girlfriend at Glastonbury that means he's in the record industry.

DD: He *is* in the record industry.

LAILA: You know what DD, think what you want I don't care. It's not important. But in my opinion people Dad's age shouldn't even be going to Glastonbury. They should leave that to us. But people like Dad and all his friends, they can't. He can't just let us be young and him be old, he has to get in on it and have the music and the clothes and the games and the phones and I think it's pathetic. He'd rather do all that than…it's pathetic. I wish they would just admit that they're not young and we are. Dress like an adult! Talk like an adult! Apologise and help us! Then maybe we could…look, this isn't important, okay. Sing your little song. I'm going to take Frankie back to ours right?

They go to leave.

DD: Laila. I told you a lie. About Ali being in Sensation Nation. I told a lie and I'm sorry.

LAILA: Yeah I know. Of course I know. She was my friend.

DD: Then why did you…?

LAILA: I was doing something nice for my sister. You got a problem with that? Good luck.

LAILA leaves. FRANKIE hands the lyric sheet back to DD and shakes her head apologetically and exits out the door after LAILA.

Pause.

JEAN BROWN: Those bastards said that if I just joined in I'd get better. So I did this. Heard you talking in the corridor and joined right in. Did it quickly too, not really, you know, thinking about it or whatever. Unbelievable really. Joined in. They were right. For once. I think. So I'll sing with you if you want. I can't be this…terrified…for nothing. There needs to be a point to feeling like this. Or else…nothing's changed. Know what I mean?

MARCY: Oh well DD it's a duet now. Things are looking up.

SEAN has been out of sight in the far corner of the room looking for his shoes again. He pops up, shoe in hand.

SEAN: Yeeeeeess!!!! Found one. It was under this curtain. And guess what? There's a door here! Check it out, look. There's a kind of door here or something – with a curtain. That's where they went. I knew they couldn't've gone into a parallel universe. There'd've been lightning flashes and thunder noises and stuff wouldn't there? Nah it was just a normal door with nothing behind it but…

SEAN opens the door to reveal JAKE SPENCE. He immediately shuts the door again.

SEAN: Ghosts.

Reactions from the others.

SEAN: Oh my actual god.

SEAN slowly opens the door again.

JAKE: Please don't…Please. I just wanted to…I dunno.

AMEE: How long have you been back there?

JAKE: Since *In The Night Garden*. There's a window down there, I climbed in, I'm not hurting anyone…

MARCY: I'm going to get Callum.

JAKE: No! Please. I'm not hurting anyone. I just want to say… no, I just want to listen. Why can't I just stay here and listen? This is the last time. This is the last chance I have. Why can't I be here?

SPOKE'S BROTHER: Because you left. You left her once, you left forever.

JAKE: But. No. You said. You said I've done nothing wrong. I heard you.

SPOKE'S BROTHER: I said you didn't kill her. Cos you didn't. But you did do something wrong. You left her.

JAKE: I couldn't…I couldn't help it. I was thrown from the car man and when I opened my eyes, I was running. Like a little kid. Running that way you used to. Full pelt. So fast. Too fast. I couldn't stop. No one could.

SPOKE'S BROTHER: I could. Because, see, the difference between you and me is that I loved her. So I couldn't've ran. You're just a guy who was there and this'll be you and her tangled together for good. You got lucky. You and her are like a tattoo now. So what? It doesn't mean you love her. Not like me. Cos I've known her since I was a kid. Her dad and my dad went to school together. This school. And I loved her. I loved her when she used to come to my house for Christmas and I loved her when we played in her garden and once it was really raining and we didn't go in. Well. I loved her then the most. They called for us to go in but we didn't. She held me back. It was raining so hard and it was all ours – this rain-world. Every night I've thought about her. Every single night. And when I got rid of…rid of…fucking…THIS! She would've loved me back. Oh yes she would. Oh yes she would.

SPOKE's BROTHER meant his body, when he said 'THIS'. He meant when he grows up. He punched himself in the chest when he said it. He screamed the word. He tears at himself a bit. Then he stops.

JAKE: I loved her too.

Pause.

SPOKE'S BROTHER: Whatever. Nothing matters. I'm going to find my family.

JAKE: Are you going to tell them? Are you?

SPOKE's BROTHER doesn't answer. He exits.

There's a big pause. The organ plays again.

DD: That's the cue.

JEAN BROWN: I'm ready.

MARCY: You're doing it?

DD: It's either that or we run.

41

NADIA: I'll do it. Too. For me I mean. If you want?

DD: Yeah. I do. I really do. Thank you Nadia. And I'm sorry. Everyone. I am. Sean, if you want to go out with Amee I don't mind. Well I mind, but…you know what I mean? I can't stop it. *(To YJB and NADIA.)* Ready?

They look terrified. Deep breaths.

JAKE: What song are you going to sing?

Nobody responds.

DD: See you on the other side.

DD, YOUNG JEAN BROWN and NADIA exit like soldiers going into battle.

AMEE: I'm going too. Sean?

SEAN: Oh my god. Amee. I…

AMEE: Sean. No.

SEAN: Right. Good.

They scuttle off, SEAN desperately putting his shoe on as he goes.

MARCY: *(As they go.)* But why? But why?

They're gone. It's just MARCY left from Sensation Nation now. After a quick beat, and a glance at JAKE, she goes after the others.

JAKE: But why?

She turns, shrugs and exits.

It's just JAKE now. Just JAKE and the candles and the crosses and the stars above him.

But when the song starts, that changes. Everything changes when the song starts…

* * *

I have no idea what song Sensation Nation sing. I really couldn't say what an eighteen-year-old girl's favourite song would be.

But you know don't you?

Think about it. Talk about it. And you'll know what's right.

Although Sensation Nation are in the main church, away from this room, I think we should see them somewhere, as they line up; ready – scared. Brave.

The cool thing they do, the thing NADIA mentioned earlier, is that seconds before they sing, they link hands.

And she was right. It is beautiful.

And it changes everything.

JAKE, when he hears the song begin and realises what it is, slowly folds up, down upon his knees, head wrapped up in his arms, crying hard for himself, like a baby.

All the junk in this room, all these relics and paraphernalia, these weird wooden icons…they go. They disappear. We don't need them now.

We have the song.

Above us, the stars and the moon which were faded and flaking before, glow. They glow and then they blossom.

The stars turn into white flowers. Flowers fall, flowers burst through every dusty and dank corner on the stage. White flowers…everywhere.

Then, all at once, the petals clear and JAKE is exactly as he was, but is no longer in some side room at a service

He's in a garden.

And the song continues…

The grass here is green and perfect. The sky is childhood blue. There are long, fake-looking daisies here and there. Strong trees let dappled summer-morning light pulse kindly on the lawn. It feels like a garden we were in once before. Years and years ago maybe. A perfect garden for children.

JAKE opens his eyes.

There's a bridge. Painted white and twinkling with tiny lights.

And standing on that bridge is ALI.

The music continues throughout, underneath this. But they aren't singing right now…

ALI: Alright mate?

JAKE: Ali?

ALI: You alright?

JAKE: This is your favourite song?

ALI: I fucking *love* this song.

JAKE: I didn't know that.

ALI: Well. It's not important.

JAKE: I think…I think it's important.

ALI: I'm telling you mate, it's not.

JAKE: I'm…I'm…oh god Ali I am so sorry. I am. I really am so fucking…

    JAKE cries.

ALI: I know man. Yeah I know you are. But it's okay.

JAKE: I'm going to kill myself or something Ali.

ALI: Nah. You're not.

JAKE: Why not? There's no reason now.

ALI: Yes there is. I'm asking you not to. It wasn't your fault man. I was driving, the other guy was overtaking in a crazy place…

JAKE: But I ran. They're right, I ran! And that's going to be *on* me for the rest of my life. What can I do now that's not running? Nothing.

ALI: Something will happen. Something good. Just wait.

JAKE: It's like I know what I'm going to be though. And it's not fair. I have to be the bad guy now. Everything I do. Imagine that. Imagine having no choice when it comes to that.

ALI: You're not a bad guy. I'm not into bad guys. I liked you cos you were funny in Physics and you were sweet to my little brother and your jeans look great. You're not bad. And anyway there's no rule I don't think, everyone can change. If you want it bad enough.

JAKE: That sounds like it's from Hollyoaks.

ALI: It *is* from Hollyoaks! Oh my god! That's something else I like about you, you're totally into Hollyoaks even though it's desperate and sad.

Pause. They smile.

JAKE: What…what's it like?

ALI: Amazing. There's another world right underneath. Like a vibration or something. Hey, see when the car flipped? Did time kind of…

JAKE: Slow…

ALI: Yeah! Like, totally slow down. Well, that's what it's like.

JAKE: What do you mean?

ALI: It's only when you get things at real-time speed – at this speed – that you realise everything's been going too fast. Too fast to see. I think we knew it was there, felt it was there, this other world, but we just couldn't see it. It was zooming by – right in front of our nose. Even photographs are travelling at the speed of light Jake, so what chance do we have? You can feel it though, like a vibration, but you can't see it. You can't see anything except the vapour trails of stuff that's long gone. Well, when the car flipped we got to see the world as it really is. Didn't we? And where I am now I see it all the time. And it's simple and it's beautiful and…yeah, I'm fine. And I'm there under everything, inside everything. I'm not gone Jake. You're just moving too fast to see me.

JAKE: I want to stay here. I'll never leave you again Ali. I swear to god. I'll never leave you.

ALI: Mate, you're going to leave me now.

JAKE: No.

ALI: Yeah.

JAKE: Why?

ALI: Because it's time to go.

ALI kisses JAKE and walks over the bridge.

Sensation Nation start singing again. The last chorus.

ALI waves goodbye.

JAKE waves back.

When she's gone the garden goes with her.

JAKE is back in the room again. The door to the congregation right in front of him.

The song finishes. Sensation Nation let go of each other's hand and go into darkness.

JAKE gets to his feet, takes a deep breath and walks through the door: forward on the tide, into the now.

The End.

NOTES ON TOO FAST

Single and group activity suggestions for students and teachers studying Douglas Maxwell's play in order to get inside the playtext and gain a thorough understanding of its story, characters, style and themes

TITLE

Why do you think Douglas Maxwell decided to call his play *Too Fast*?

Make a list of all the reasons you think led him to do this.

Discuss the reasons you have arrived at. Do you think it's more satisfying for a play to have a title which can have several meanings, and reflects different aspects of the play? What other titles could he have given his play?

You may wish to design a poster for a production of the play, thinking carefully about which images and words to use in order to tantalize a potential audience and make them curious to see the play.

On the poster, you are allowed to put one sentence under the title, explaining what the play is about: what is that sentence?

LOCATION

Apart from the magical ending of the play, most of the action happens in the side-room of a church, and the audience is continually reminded of the funeral which is taking place in the main part of the church next-door by the comments the characters make, as they come and go, and peer through the connecting door.

Why do you think the writer chose to set the play in one location, having characters coming in and out, rather than using several locations? What effect does this have on the audience watching the play?

Douglas Maxwell describes the room in quite a lot of detail. Find images of rooms like this, and photos of objects you think may be seen in the room. Collect them together, and put them on the wall so that you can look at them and think about them as a group. Do you think the overall image of the room could be a metaphor for the story of *Too Fast*? Explain your answer in as much detail as you can.

STORY

The story of *Too Fast* is very simple. A girl has been killed in a road accident, and the boy who may have been responsible turns up at her funeral. The main actions that happen in the play are the arrival of Jake Spence and his re-union with Ali. All other action has either already happened or happens offstage and is reported by the characters onstage.

Choose your favourite character from the play and write his or her diary from the day of the accident to the day of the funeral. Make sure it's faithful to what you know from the play, and be as inventive and detailed as you like when imagining things that are not contained in the script.

CHARACTERS

Spoke's Brother is the youngest of the characters we meet. The members of Sensation Nation are aged between 14-16. Callum Hunt, Laila, Frankie, Jake and Ali are all aged 16-18.

How do the younger characters differ from the older characters? Do you notice differences in the way they speak? Do they respond to events differently? How do the ways they value certain things differ?

Almost every character remembers things from the past – do the older characters remember things in a different way to the younger characters?

Some characters say a lot, and some say very little. Identify which are which.

Some characters repeat things a lot: what effect does this have?

Compare the characters in the play with the members of your class: do you notice any similarities?

Have a look at the front cover of this book. Which characters do you think are in the photograph?

STATUS

Read through the play noticing which characters are bossy and order other characters about. Which characters tend to do as they're told and which ones ask questions and put up a fight? Would you describe any of them as bullies? Do you think any of them enjoy playing 'victim'?

Do the levels of status between the characters alter depending on who is in the room?

Examine the language used by characters to describe, argue and persuade. Choose some examples, and write about how the characters use language very skillfully to make their point, win an argument and get what they want.

TELEVISION PROGRAMMES

Everyone in the play has a shared knowledge of entertainment programmes which have been broadcast on television and targeted at children. All of these characters are now in their teens, and look back on the television of their childhood with a range of opinions. Identify and discuss some of these opinions by comparing them to how you remember your earliest on-screen entertainment. Did you learn anything? Do you still enjoy the programmes? Are you embarrassed by them, or bored by them? If so, why?

SWEARING

Young Jean Brown enjoys seizing everybody's attention by deliberately using words which cause offence. How does she go about doing this? Why do certain words provoke extreme reactions in some listeners? What does this tell us about Young Jean Brown, and what do you imagine her background to be?

Can you think of words which you wouldn't use at home or in school, but that you would use among friends of the same age?

What is the difference between swearing and slang?

Does swearing change depending on age groups that use it? Do you think certain swear words fall in and out of fashion?

THE SONG

Ali Monroe's favourite song is sung by Sensation Nation at the end of the play. Douglas Maxwell has deliberately left it to the reader or the company performing the play to imagine which song it is.

Which song do you think Ali would have liked it to be? Which song do you think DD and her group would choose? Make a list of all the potential songs, and discuss reasons why you have chosen each one.

THEMES

Look back at the work you did examining the title of *Too Fast*.

What would you say are the play's main themes? Make a list of them, with an explanation of each one.

What do you think is the play's central theme?

What did the play make you think about when you read it for the first time? Did you make connections with events in your own childhood, or teenage years? If so, what were they, and did these connections lead to you having a more vivid response to the play?

Douglas Maxwell's play is both hilariously funny and extremely sad and moving. What is the effect of the combination of those two reactions?

What do you think an audience will think about as they leave the theatre, after a performance of *Too Fast*?

OTHER DOUGLAS MAXWELL TITLES

Decky Does a Bronco
£7.99 / 9781840022438

Helmet
£7.99 / 9781840022759

If Destroyed True
£7.99 / 9781840025637

Mancub
£7.99 / 9781840024753

Melody
£8.99 / 9781840026634

Miracle Man
£8.99 / 9781849430326

The Mother Ship
£8.99 / 9781840028331

Our Bad Magnet
£7.99 / 9781840022445

Promises Promises
£8.99 / 9781849430647

Variety
£7.99 / 9781840023312

New collection coming soon:

Douglas Maxwell: Plays for Young People
Decky Does a Bronco, Helmet, Mancub, The Mother Ship and *Too Fast*
£12.99 / 9781849431507 / June 2012

WWW.OBERONBOOKS.COM

Follow us on www.twitter.com/@oberonbooks
& www.facebook.com/oberonbook